Intersections
SMALL GROUP SERIES

Faith

Confidence and Doubt in Daily Life

Martin E. Marty

Augsburg Fortress, Minneapolis

Contents

INTERSECTIONS
Small Group Series

Faith
Confidence and Doubt in Daily Life

Developed in cooperation with the Division for Congregational Ministries

George W. Johnson, series introduction
David W. Anderson and Carolyn F. Lystig, editors
The Wells Group, series design
Sylvia Schlender, cover photo

Quotations identified as *BC* are from *The Book of Concord,* translated and edited by Theodore G. Tappert, copyright © 1959 Fortress Press.

Scripture quotations are from New Revised Standard Version Bible, copyright 1989 Division of Christian Education of the National Council of the Churches of Christ in the United States of America. Used by permission.

Introduction

Seasons of life

We are going to talk about faith as it matches the seasons of life. Seasons of life can mean a long time—childhood, adulthood, being elderly are all far apart. However, we also want to know how to get through today. Seasons of life can mean its moods and situations. What does faith have to do with my ordinary, day-to-day life?

When we get up in the morning, there is an uncharted day ahead. Most of us carry over some guilt from yesterday. *Christian faith says we need not, we should not.* Most of us greet the day with some worry about tomorrow. *Christian faith says we should not, we need not.*

All of us will face problems that will be too big to face alone. *Christian faith says God can be with us, God is with us.*

As we grow in faith, we shall be more ready to meet what the day brings, in confidence and hope, and with readiness for the practical details.

Making your way

This course is about confidence and doubt in daily life, about making our way through the seasons of life. Each day of life, and all of life taken together, looks like a maze, a labyrinth. That is, we enter it at a certain door called birth and exit it at one named death—or, in faith, one that could be named "Access to Eternal Life." Between the two, *anything* can happen. Since anything can happen we should prepare for it, for *anything* certainly will happen.

Remember—this is all about your life, my life, not someone else's, not humanity in general. How do we face the maze?

Facing the maze

Sometimes at our house we play a game: you must choose someone else, now alive, that you would like to be if you cannot be you. (That's the hard rule: You cannot be you. You cannot refuse to play, or we won't serve coffee and cake at the end of the party.)

This person you choose may be beautiful, wealthy, and famous. But you have to take on all of his or her liabilities along with the assets. You have to share the moral perplexities, the habits, the disappointments and doubts and ambiguities of such a person. Most people, you will find, will have a hard time coming up with the name of any one of the six billion choices of people open to them.

From the past

Ask them about someone from the past that they would like to have been and more will play, play willingly, and come up with choices. Why? Not because these people did not have disappointments, doubts, or moral confusions and a bad record. It is simply that when a life is over, we can run a balance sheet on it. We say: Yes, the torment she went through as an artist or a mother was worth it—look at the works of genius or the children in which she can take pride!

What's the difference?

We know how to treat the one who has been through the entire maze, the labyrinth of life. We do not know what will come of the one lost in it. We are such persons, right in the midst of life. We take many wrong turns, run into blind alleys, come to dead ends, circle in cul-de-sacs as often as we find an opening to something promising. Yet even then, it is hard to foresee what is next.

Who would have thought it?

When we can read hundreds of obituaries and biographies we have to say in almost every case: Who would have thought it? Who would have thought that the rail-splitter in Kentucky and Illinois would become the greatest president of the United States? Who could have foreseen in his maze that his life would suddenly end with an assassination?

We can foresee certain things about some people. Those who enter the maze desperately poor have a hard time coming out rich; few do. Children of royalty often have their royal jobs cut out for them. But what we know about them suggests that there is a maze in their cases, too.

The bottom line

Here's the bottom line: Faith is important for finding a way through the labyrinth. No one, least of all biblical writers, suggests that faith is sight, that it represents the end of the story when everything has been made clear. Faith is "the assurance of things hoped for, the conviction of things not seen" (Hebrews 1:1).

If the hopes were realized, we would not need faith. Someday, according to the Bible, we will not need it. Only love is forever. If the things were seen, we would not need faith. While faith can be strengthened by "things seen," it cannot depend on them. We see too many things that distract us or that could defeat faith based on sight.

Danger: False advertising

So it is dangerous to overadvertise what faith can do. In our world, shaped by the market as it is, many people turn faith into a commodity. One walks into a virtual supermarket of faith in modern America. Picture the appeals: "Buy my book about faith and it will solve all your problems." "Believe in the God within you, the God that you are, and you will have self-esteem and will win in life." "Here are 10 easy steps by which you can overcome your doubts and be assured of success."

All that is false advertising. Are the people who invent the programs, write the books, run the retreats, people who live by sight, seeing and realizing everything? Why do so many of them need therapy? Why are there so many competing solutions for sale in the mall and marketplace?

Serious searchers

Small groups are helpful for you who are serious searchers, who want to understand faith. By telling each other your stories, or discussing what the Bible says about faith, you can help criticize false claims. You and other members of your group, without being snoopy or personal, will make suggestions, offer solutions to problems, feel free to discuss issues that trouble you, and, in short, find and help build faith in each other and meet other people in confident ways.

In your small group study of *Faith: Confidence and Doubt in Daily Life,* may you find partners in a conversation that will help make God's presence felt among you and in your daily lives.

SMALL GROUP SERIES

Welcome into the family of those who are part of small groups! Intersections Small Group Series will help you and other members of your group build relationships and discover ways to connect the Christian faith with your everyday life.

This book is prepared for those who want to make a difference in this world, who want to grow in their Christian faith, as well as for those who are beginning to explore the Christian faith. The information in this introduction to the Intersections small group experience can help your group make the most out of your time together.

Biblical encouragement

"Do not be conformed to this world, but be transformed by the renewing of your minds, so that you may discern what is the will of God—what is good and acceptable and perfect" (Romans 12:2).

Small groups provide an atmosphere where the Holy Spirit can transform lives. As you share your life stories and learn together, God's Spirit can work to enlighten and direct you.

Strength is provided to face the pressures to conform to forces and influences that are opposed to what is "good and acceptable and perfect." To "be transformed" is an ongoing experience of God's grace as we take up the cross and follow Jesus. Changed lives happen as we live in community with one another. Small groups encourage such change and growth.

What is a small group?

A number of definitions and descriptions of the small group ministry experience exist throughout the church. Roberta Hestenes, a Presbyterian pastor and author, defines a small group as an intentional face-to-face gathering of three to twelve people who meet regularly with the common purpose of discovering and growing in the possibilities of the abundant life.

Whatever definition you use, the following characteristics are important.

Small—Seven to ten people is ideal so that everyone can be heard and no one's voice is lost. More than 12 members makes genuine caring difficult.

Intentional—Commitment to the group is a high priority.

Personal—Sharing experiences and insights is more important than mastering content.

Conversational—Leaders that facilitate conversation, rather than teach, are the key to encouraging participation.

Friendly—Having a warm, accepting, non-judgmental atmosphere is essential.

Christ-centered—The small group experience is biblically based, related to the real world, and founded on Christ.

Features of Intersections Small Group Series

A small group model

A number of small group ministry models exist. Most models include three types of small groups:

- *Discipleship groups*—where people gather to grow in Christian faith and life;

- *Support and recovery group*s—which focus on special interests, concerns, or needs; and

- *Ministry groups*—which have a task-oriented focus.

Intersections Small Group Series presently offers material for discipleship groups and support and recovery groups.

For discipleship groups, this series offers a variety of courses with Bible study at the center. What makes a discipleship group different from traditional group Bible studies? In discipleship groups, members bring their life experience to the exploration of the biblical material.

For support and recovery groups, Intersections Small Group Series offers topical material to assist group members in dealing with issues related to their common experience, hurt, or interest. An extra section of facilitator helps in the back of the book will assist leaders of support and recovery groups to anticipate and prepare for special circumstances and needs that may arise as group members explore a topic.

Ministry groups can benefit from an environment that includes prayer, biblical reflection, and relationship building, in addition to their task focus.

Four essentials

Prayer, personal sharing, biblical reflection, and a group ministry task are part of each time you gather. These are all important for Christian community to be experienced. Each of the six chapter themes in each book includes:

- Short prayers to open and close your time together.

- Carefully worded questions to make personal sharing safe, non-threatening, and voluntary.

- A biblical base from which to understand and discover the power and grace of God. God's Word is the compass that keeps the group on course.

- A group ministry task to encourage both individuals and the group as a whole to find ways to put faith into action.

Flexibility

Each book contains six chapter themes that may be covered in six sessions or easily extended for groups that meet for a longer period of time. Each chapter theme is organized around two to three main topics with supplemental material to make it easily adaptable to your small group's needs. You need not use all the material. Most themes will work well for 1½- to 2-hour sessions, but a variety of scheduling options is possible.

Bible based

Each of the six chapter themes in the book includes one or more Bible texts printed in its entirety from the New Revised Standard Version of the Bible. This makes it easy for all group members to read and learn from the same text. Participants will be encouraged through questions, with exercises, and by other group members to address biblical texts in the context of their own lives.

User friendly

The material is prepared in such a way that it is easy to follow, practical, and does not require a professional to lead it. Designating one to be the facilitator to guide the group is important, but there is no requirement for this person to be theologically trained or an expert in the course topic. Many times options are given so that no one will feel forced into any set way of responding.

Group goals and process

1. **Creating a group covenant or contract for your time together will be important.** During your first meeting, discuss these important characteristics of all small groups and decide how your group will handle them.

Confidentiality—Agreeing that sensitive issues that are shared remain in the group.

Regular attendance—Agreeing to make meetings a top priority.

Non-judgmental behavior—Agreeing to confess one's own shortcomings, if appropriate, not those of others, and not giving advice unless asked for it.

Prayer and support—Being sensitive to one another, listening, becoming a caring community.

Accountability—Being responsible to each other and open to change.

Items in your covenant should be agreed upon by all members. Add to the group covenant as you go along. Space to record key aspects is included in the back of this book. See page 60.

2. **Everyone is responsible for the success of the group, but do arrange to have one facilitator who can guide the group process each time you meet.**

The facilitator is not a teacher or healer. Teaching, learning, and healing happen from the group experience. The facilitator is more of a shepherd who leads the flock to where they can feed and drink and feel safe.

Remember, an important goal is to experience genuine love and community in a Christ-centered atmosphere. To help make this happen, the facilitator encourages active listening and honest sharing. This person allows the material to facilitate opportunities for self-awareness and interaction with others.

Leadership is shared in a healthy group, but the facilitator is the one designated to set the pace, keep the group focused, and enable the members to support and care for each other.

People need to sense trust and freedom as the group develops; therefore, avoid "shoulds" or "musts" in your group.

3. **Taking on a group ministry task can help members of your group balance personal growth with service to others.**

In your first session, identify ways your group can offer help to others within the congregation or in your surrounding community. Take time at each meeting to do or arrange for that ministry task. Many times it is in the doing that we discover what we believe or how God is working in our lives.

4. **Starting or continuing a personal action plan offers a way to address personal needs that you become aware of in your small group experience.**

For example, you might want to spend more time in conversation with a friend or spouse. Your action plan might state, "I plan to visit with Terry two times before our next small group meeting."

If you decide to pursue a personal action plan, consider sharing it with your small group. Your group can be helpful in at least three ways: by giving support; helping to define the plan in realistic, measurable ways; and offering a source to whom you can be accountable.

5. **Prayer is part of small group fellowship.** There is great power in group prayer, but not everyone feels free to offer spontaneous prayer. That's okay.

Learning to pray aloud takes time and practice. If you feel uncomfortable, start with simple and short prayers. And remember to pray for other members between sessions.

Use page 61 in the back of this book to note prayer requests made by group members.

6. **Consider using a journal to help reflect on your experiences and insights between meeting times.**

Writing about feelings, ideas, and questions can be one way to express yourself; plus it helps you remember what so often gets lost with time.

The "Daily Walk" component includes material that can get your journaling started. This, of course, is up to you and need not be done on any regular schedule. Even doing it once a week can be time well spent.

How to use this book

The material provided for each session is organized around some key components. If you are the facilitator for your small group, be sure to read this section carefully.

The facilitator's role is to establish a hospitable atmosphere and set a tone that encourages participants to share, reflect, and listen to each other. Some important practical things can help make this happen.

- Whenever possible meet in homes. Be sure to provide clear directions about how to get there.

- Use name tags for several sessions.

- Place the chairs in a circle and close enough for everyone to hear and feel connected.

- Be sure everyone has access to a book; preparation will pay off.

Welcoming

A hospitable atmosphere is critical to the success of your small group. Many of us are timid about expressing ourselves. We may fear that our ignorance about details of faith may be exposed and we will be embarrassed. Yet there is something about faith in God, and about the act of talking about faith, that builds confidence

A spirit of hospitality makes it easier to build the confidence to speak about faith. It makes it easier to share our stories, raise our questions, and express both our confidence and doubt.

The use of name tags for the first few sessions and the presence of light refreshments are examples of the little extras that make entering and sharing in the group easier. Pay attention to lighting; comfortable seating where you can see one another; soothing versus harsh sounds and music; and a sense of privacy for caring conversations.

Focus

Each of the six chapter themes in this book has a brief focus statement. Read it aloud. It will give everyone a sense of the direction for each session and provide some boundaries so that people will not feel lost or frustrated trying to cover everything. The focus also connects the theme to the course topic.

Community building

This opening activity is crucial to a relaxed, friendly atmosphere. It will prepare the ground for gradual group development. Two "Community Building" options are provided under each theme. With the facilitator giving his or her response to the questions first, others are free to follow.

One purpose for this section is to allow everyone to participate as he or she responds to non-threatening questions. The activity serves as a check-in time when participants are invited to share how things are going or what is new.

Make this time light and fun; remember, humor is a welcome gift. Use 15 to 20 minutes for this activity in your first few sessions and keep the entire group together.

During your first meeting, encourage group members to write down names and phone numbers (when appropriate) of the other members, so people can keep in touch. Use page 59 for this purpose.

Discovery

This component focuses on exploring the theme for your time together, using material that is read, and questions and exercises that encourage sharing of personal insights and experiences.

Reading material includes a Bible text with supplemental passages and commentary written by the topic writer. Have volunteers read the Bible texts aloud. Read the commentary aloud only when it seems helpful. The main passage to be used is printed so that everyone operates from a common translation and sees the text.

"A Further Look" is included in some places to give you additional study material if time permits. Use it to explore related passages and questions. Be sure to have your own Bible handy.

Questions and exercises related to the theme will invite personal sharing and storytelling. Keep in mind that as you listen to each other's stories, you are inspired to live more fully in the grace and will of God. Such exchanges make Christianity relevant and transformation more likely to happen. Caring relationships are key to clarifying one's beliefs. Sharing personal experiences and insights is what makes the small group spiritually satisfying.

Most people are open to sharing their life stories, especially if they're given permission to do so and they know someone will actively listen. Starting with the facilitator's response usually works best. On some occasions you may want to break the group into units of three or four persons to explore certain questions. When you reconvene, relate your experience to the whole group. The phrase "Explore and Relate," which appears occasionally in the margin, refers to this recommendation. Encourage couples to separate for this smaller group activity. Appoint someone to start the discussion.

Wrap-up

Plan your schedule so that there will be enough time for wrapping up. This time can include work on your group ministry task, review of key discoveries during your time together, identifying personal and prayer concerns, closing prayers, and the Lord's Prayer.

The facilitator can help the group identify and plan its ministry task. Introduce the idea and decide on your group ministry task during "Wrap-up" time in the first session. Tasks need not be grandiose. Activities might include:

- Ministry in your community, such as "adopting" a food shelf, clothes closet, or homeless shelter; sponsoring equipment, food, or clothing drives; or sending members to staff the shelter.

- Ministry to members of the congregation, such as writing notes to those who are ill or bereaved.

- Congregational tasks where volunteers are always needed, such as serving refreshments during the fellowship time after worship, stuffing envelopes for a church mailing, or taking responsibility for altar preparations for one month.

Depending upon the task, you can use part of each meeting time to carry out or plan the task.

In the "Wrap-up," allow time for people to share insights and encouragements and to voice special prayer requests. Just to mention someone who needs prayer is a form of prayer. The "Wrap-up" time may include a brief worship experience with candles, prayers, and singing. You might form a circle and hold hands. Silence can be effective. If you use the Lord's Prayer in your group, select the version that is known in your setting. There is space on page 62 to record the version your group uses. Another closing prayer is also printed on page 62. Before you go, ask members to pray for one another during the week. Remember also any special concerns or prayer requests.

Daily walk

Seven Bible readings and a thought, prayer, and verse for the journey related to the material just discussed are provided for those who want to keep the theme before them between sessions. These brief readings may be used for devotional time. Some group members may want to memorize selected passages. The Bible readings can also be used for supplemental study by the group if needed. Prayer for other group members can also be part of this time of personal reflection.

A word of encouragement

No material is ever complete or perfect for every situation or group. Creativity and imagination will be important gifts for the facilitator to bring to each theme. Keep in mind that it is in community that we are challenged to grow in Jesus Christ. Together we become what we could not become alone. It is God's plan that it be so.

For additional resources and ideas see *Starting Small Groups—and Keeping Them Going* (Minneapolis: Augsburg Fortress, 1995).

1 Faith for Seasons of Beginnings

Focus

Trust is a faith for the seasons of beginnings. Let's focus on the nature and dynamics of childlike faith in God who is trustworthy.

Community building

For setting small group goals, see page 7.

List your goals and commitments in the appendix on page 60 for future reference.

Think of an experience concerning faith and trust and share this with the group.

Maybe it's a positive or negative experience.

Maybe it's a serious or funny story.

Maybe it happened when you were a child or an adult.

Maybe it happened to you or to someone else.

Maybe it's something you learned or discovered.

It need not be profound; it could even be silly.

Option

Share with the group a childhood experience of faith or trust in a parent or older acquaintance who helped you overcome a fear or difficulty.

For example, Dad or Mom calming you as a child after having a nightmare, or big brother helping you ride a bicycle for the first time.

Opening prayer

Dear God, let the faith of a child, simple and confident, become a part of my search, through Jesus Christ, who gave the example of such faith and who commended it to us. Amen.

Luke 18:17

17 "Truly I tell you, whoever does not receive the kingdom of God as a little child will never enter it."

Think about it

The late comic actor W. C. Fields, when caught reading the Bible as he was convalescing in a hospital, replied that he was just looking for loopholes. Maybe we all do that. We might look for loopholes when we do not like a command of God. If we find something hard to swallow, we also look for loopholes. Do we need one when we hear from Jesus that we have to enter the kingdom of God "as a little child?"

A trusting child

The text is so charming that there seem to be no reasons to look for a way around it. Magazine covers with children on them sell well. Grandparents show pictures of their cute grandchildren. We like a story in which Jesus blesses infants and honors parents—"family values"! So what is the problem?

The problem is this: We spend years trying to get past beginnings, to grow up. And then we hear: "Receive the kingdom of God as a little child." Impossible! Unhealthy! Who can think her way into the wondrous and terrifying world of the child? "Grow up!" "Act your age!" "Get counseling so you can mature!" But Jesus asks us to become "as a little child." What is going on?

If we want to take this text straight, we assume there is something about children, some quality, that can be healthful for adults, all life long. There is. The commentators agree that this word about children is really an invitation to trust. Psychologist Erik Erikson tells us the most important thing that a child has, or should have, is "basic trust."

In God we trust

Christian faith wants us to have "basic trust," which means that we are to see God as trustworthy. However, trust is more than a concept; it is based on human experiences

Discuss as a group.

- Let's start with simple stories. No one has to reveal deep, dark secrets, but can you tell about childhood experiences that led you to *trust* adults?

■ What about some expriences that led you to mistrust the adult world?

Read and discuss.

Consider this

If God promises to be supportive but lets us go; if God gives us tests so extreme that we do not feel the divine hand, then there is danger that we will be insecure, shaky, unready to try new ventures of faith.

"Faith is a vital, deliberate trust in God's grace, so certain that it would die a thousand times for it." *BC* 553.12

■ **What is encouraging about the faith and trust expressed in this quote?**

■ **What is challenging?**

Idolatry

Biblical writers always show God being concerned lest we humans put our trust in the wrong place; they call it idolatry or foolishness.

Idolatry need not mean worshiping a shelf full of images. It might mean trusting money, securities, possessions, career.

Someone could supply a pile of papers and magazines and the group can go looking right on the spot; you do not need many to find examples.

■ Look for advertisements with photographs that depict people putting their trust in the wrong things.

■ Discuss examples from business, entertainment, or athletic sections of newspapers. What is the problem?

Discuss as a group.

Consider this

The people in a midwestern farming community were experiencing a bad summer drought. The pastor gathered them together in his church to pray for long-awaited rain. The church was full and the prayers were long, but one person, a little girl, bothered to bring *an umbrella!*

■ **How does this story help us to understand childlike faith?**

Trust

Explore and relate.
Explore in groups of three or four; then *relate* a brief summary to the entire group.

Reflect on these images and portraits of God.

a. Grand old man
b. Managing director
c. God of our parents
d. A loving God
e. Kind shepherd
f. Resident policeman
g. A gracious friend
h. Heavenly Father
i. A compassionate mother
j. A rock and refuge
k. Other

- Which ones have helped you in your faith and why?

- In which images are you most likely to have the greatest sense of trust?

- Which ones have hindered you in your faith and why?

A further look

Divide into three groups, each taking one of the Scriptures and questions. Share your insights with the larger group.

- Read Galatians 4:1-7. How does one stop being a "slave" and become a child of inheritance?

- Read 1 Corinthians 1:26-31. Why does Paul put such a premium on being weak, low, and "foolish?"

- Read Acts 16: 25-34. Can one be brought to faith with a few simple words, as this text seems to suggest?

Discovery

If this study theme is used for more than one small group session, introduce subsequent sessions with a "Community Builder" and "Opening Prayer" and end with "Wrap-up."

Ephesians 4:14-15

14 We must no longer be children, tossed to and fro and blown about by every wind of doctrine. . . . 15But speaking the truth in love, we must grow up in every way into him who is the head, into Christ.

Growing pains

The child trusts the mother and father for care, just as the believer trusts God. Yet trust is not blind or stupid. Through the early years the child meets many tests. Just as the best football players are put up against the other toughest players in practice to develop strength, so children who are growing in faith will also meet tough tests.

We are to grow. Faith is a gift; we say it is a "grace." The Bible talks about growing in grace. In this letter to new Christians at Ephesus, we are told to "grow up in every way . . . into Christ." Those believers must often have been tempted to wish that they could remain "as a child" in all of life. They could not, and should not.

What stunts growth?

Our world is like that of the people at Ephesus. The writer was worried lest we, like children, be "tossed to and fro by every wind of doctrine," by people's trickery, and by their craftiness in deceitful scheming.

Such tossing, tricking, deceiving, and scheming still go on. We all know instances of people who were victims of con artists in con games.

As for doctrines—we may not call them that—all kinds of belief systems deceive people. Think of the millions of Christians who were supposed to be mature but who put childlike trust in Hitler, in Nazism; in Lenin, in communism. These leaders promoted doctrines that misled those who would grow to maturity in Christ.

Discuss as a group.

And there are new religious teachings that lead us "to and fro." Look at the "Religion/Inspiration/Self-Help/Spirituality/Metaphysical/Occult" section of your nearest popular bookstore. There will be scores if not hundreds of books full of doctrines that ask for trust—trust in the author, the stars in astrology, the crystals in New Age thought, the pop psychology in many self-help schemes.

As a group, pool experiences from what has been seen on television, heard about on radio, read about in magazines or books, or heard talked about by acquaintances.

- What are some of the doctrines that are very marketable and that attract large numbers of followers these days?

- Which popular doctrines are you most suspicious of?

To follow these quick schemes, says the letter to Ephesus, is to be deceived. They prevent the believer from growing.

Grow up . . . into Christ

You may want to read Ephesians 4:11-32 to get more details for discussion.

Try to put together a picture of a "mature" Christian, who (a) keeps showing childlike trust as a dimension of faith but (b) meets the tests of growing up and moving forward.

- What kind of personality are we likely to see?

- What kind of action might we expect of such a person?

- How does this text from Ephesians help us think about maturity?

We cannot assume that maturity is a goal in today's world, whether it be in the church or society.

■ Why is it important to "grow up . . . into Christ"?

Choose one and explain.

a. It takes mature, spiritual adults to raise maturing, faithful children.

✝ b. In our chaotic and hedonistic times, we need an inner compass of mature faith to survive emotionally, relationally, and spiritually.

c. We can easily deceive ourselves to pursue personal wants that are neither healthy nor faithful.

✝ d. Attitudes and actions are so violent in today's world that we need to be renewed daily with the peace that passes understanding.

e. We are God's instruments of hope for a despairing world.

f. Other.

A further look

■ Read Isaiah 6:6-9. Why should we keep seeking to grow in faith if we also may not understand much anyhow?

■ Read Colossians 1:21-23. How does one become securely established and steadfast in faith?

Discovery

Psalm 52:8

8 **But I am like a green olive tree
in the house of God.
I trust in the steadfast love of God
forever and ever.**

What trust means

The book of Psalms often talks about what trust means, about why to trust, and about how trusting people are to be. Here a picture from nature describes someone who trusts. The green olive tree, full of life and possibility, is the image of the one who can say, "I trust in the steadfast love of God."

The steadfast love of God: that word *steadfast love* ("chesed" in Hebrew) appears often in the Old Testament. It becomes crucial now as we talk about trust during the developing stages of life and faith. The importance of people needing to trust is pointless unless the object, the focus of trust merits our trust.

Have an assigned person bring in some pictures that remind us of suffering: people in cancer wards or with AIDS; people cleaning up after a disaster.

Talk about these cases in which the steadfast love of God does not seem to be present.

Discuss as a group.

The Bible is an exciting book; its writers create questions that will puzzle us long after we are children. Some people are arrogant enough to claim that they have solved all the puzzles of life; we don't trust them. They try to overlook actions in God's world that stun us—the death of children; the outbreak of wars; the alienation of someone who refuses to return our love; earthquakes; the shifting of the ground under our moral life. The Bible does not slide past any of these. Psalms is full of references to setbacks, disappointments, near despair. But through it all, the character of God as the one who shows steadfast love is the consistent theme of the whole book.

■ What do you say to people who suffer? How do you relate to them?

■ What human responses have helped/not helped during times of suffering?

Those who minister to people who are terminally ill and suffer pain say that in the overwhelming majority of cases, those who have reason to cry out and lose faith are instead more ready to trust the "steadfast love" of God—and to experience it—than are those who are in control of their life, feeling no pain.

■ What is it about situations of suffering that lead many to find more trust, deeper faith? Are they responding out of fear of hell and wanting to be on God's side, or is more happening here?

■ Share some "good circumstances" in which the love of God was evident. How can these examples encourage the attitude of trust for you?

■ Psalm 52:8 is part of a larger prayer. How is prayer part of a trusting relationship with God?

■ If you have been so led to show trust in the "steadfast love" of God when that love is not always visible or in easy reach, please tell how and why.

■ How does drawing on the support of others who care and pray help you?

A further look

■ Read Galatians 5:13-18. How does one grow into "freedom" and still respond to God's will?

■ Read Jeremiah 29:10-14. How does one go about "searching" for God?

■ Read Hebrews 11:8-12. How do Abraham and Sarah work as models for faith in our own time and place?

Wrap-up

See page 10 in the introduction for a description of "Wrap-up."

Before you go, take time for the following:

- ■ Group ministry task

- ■ Review

- ■ Personal concerns and prayer concerns

- ■ Closing prayers

Ongoing prayer requests can be listed on page 61. See page 62 for suggested closing prayers.

Daily walk

Bible readings

Day 1
Matthew 6:25-33

Day 2
Matthew 8:5-13

Day 3
Matthew 8:23-27

Day 4
Matthew 9:2-8

Day 5
Matthew 9:18-22

Day 6
Matthew 14:28-34

Day 7
Matthew 15:21-28

Thought for the journey

Christian faith is not a matter of gaining personal power and control, but of trusting the steadfast love of God in our lives and in our world.

Prayer for the journey

Lord, help us to focus on felt needs within our group, our churches, and our community. Strengthen our trust and faith in you. In Jesus' name. Amen.

Verse for the journey

"But strive first for the kingdom of God and his righteousness, and all these things will be given to you as well" (Matthew 6:33).

2 Faith for Seasons of Risk

Believing in God means taking a risk to be grounded in the deepest reality there is.

Community building

With the many demands on our lives these days, it is often difficult to accomplish the daily tasks and goals we set for ourselves.

- Share a hurdle you had to overcome to make it to your small group today.
- Name an expectation or hope you have for your group that gave you energy and motivation to be here.

Option

Share a risk you have taken that others thought you should not do and yet resulted in positive consequences for your life and/or others.

Have you taken a risk that did not work out the way you wanted?

Were you gald you tried it anyway?

Opening prayer
O God, as I believe in you, whom Jesus called Father, let me find your will revealed in his works and ways. Amen.

John 12:44

44 Then Jesus cried aloud: "Whoever believes in me believes not in me but in him who sent me."

Faith in what?

It is easy to get the impression that faith simply offers security. It is a helpful attitude to possess, a nice object to own, like a new car or a diploma. But as we make our way through the seasons of life, it becomes clear that the mere attitude of faith is useless. We have to believe in something—the United States, our company, ourself. These may not be bad things to believe in, but are they enough? Their limits are obvious. Try holding to them when lying awake at three in the morning when you think about how small you are, how short life is, how risky a business living can be.

Faith in Jesus / Faith in God

The Apostles' Creed begins, "I believe in God, the Father almighty, creator of heaven and earth."

Christians say, "Believe in Jesus!" Long ago, disciples and seekers came to Jesus and showed faith in him. Then one day he "proclaimed aloud," reminding them that faith in him was faith in God. This God he called Father, we call Creator, or Lord. Therefore, Jesus could say, "Whoever believes in me actually believes in him who sent me." Christians talk about "belief in" this one when they start their creed, "I believe in God, the Father almighty, creator of heaven and earth." Believing in God means taking a risk that you become grounded in the deepest reality there is. *Deepest reality* is a cold word. Believing in God is believing in a *person*— that is, someone who addresses us and is addressed by us.

Find a flag

Explore as a group.

Find a flag and pledge allegiance to it, salute it, or in informal language tell what it means.

- How does pledging build group spirit? How does this action represent an American or a Canadian creed?

- How does this act of pledging spread a sense of security?

- Describe the limits of what the flag can offer to people seeking meaning in life.

The Creed

■ Say together the first line of the Creed (p. 20). Does reciting the creed, telling of belief in God, when you are in a group, make faith more credible? Do you also have to risk being alone with God for the reality to sink in? Explain.

■ What if you are in a group that believes something, but you do not go along with the belief? Is it good faith to recite its creed?

■ Why did Jesus call God the one who "sent me"?

■ According to this text, what is Jesus saying to people who must have just wanted to worship Jesus?

A further look

■ Read John 1:14-18. How do we "see" God when we see Jesus, and how do we "see" Jesus? What can we learn about the mercy, justice, and compassion of God?

■ Read John 8:12-20. How has the coming of Jesus brought God closer to us and us closer to God?

Discovery

John 11:27

27 She said to him, "Yes, Lord, I believe that you are the Messiah, the Son of God, the one coming into the world."

Do you really believe?

Christians who say "I believe in God" go on to say something like, "I believe in Jesus Christ, God's only Son, our Lord." In this story, Jesus comes to console the sister of a friend who has just died. Belief in Jesus means belief that our physical death does not end our relation with God. So Jesus asked this woman named Martha whether she believed that her brother would rise again. She said yes, someday; but she got no comfort from her answer. Then Jesus said, "I am the resurrection and the life" (John 11:25). That changed everything. She then added that she believed Jesus was the one God appointed, God anointed, God called the "Son."

Believing that her brother would rise did less good than risking belief in Jesus as the resurrection and the life. Now she found comfort and strength for her daily life. She could enjoy a new relationship with her sister and have good news to spread.

Remember, if this study theme is used for more than one small group session, introduce subsequent sessions with "Community Building" and "Opening Prayer" and end with "Wrap-up."

This portion of Scripture is about what happens to relationships when Jesus helps the woman shift from "believing that" something will happen to "believing in" someone, in this case Jesus. It is also about how this relationship based on "believing in" led her to action, which meant approaching her sister and setting up an interview with Jesus.

Famous people

Respond as a group.

Together, make a list of famous people in the past.

- Take turns saying, "I believe that (for example, Julius Caesar, or William Shakespeare) lived."

- Now say, "I believe in Julius Caesar," or William Shakespeare. See what a difference that makes. No one "believes in" these dead characters.

- Now say, "I believe that Jesus lived."

- But don't stop there. Now say, "I believe in Jesus."

Discuss how you understand the difference between "that" and "in" when faith comes up. You cannot believe in a dead person; saying you believe in Jesus means you can have relationships and interactions with him now.

- What is the difference between belief that and belief in, in the case of Jesus?

Martha and Mary

Martha immediately went to Mary and said privately, "The Teacher is here and is calling for you" (John 11:28; the story does not tell us that Jesus was calling for her). Although faith is a gift from God, it often comes to us through human channels of grace.

- Share examples of believing on the basis of what someone trustworthy communicates through word and deed.

- Does the credibility of the one who tells, the one who testifies, make a difference for your faith? Explain.

Picturing Jesus

Discuss as a group.

What are some things you can picture going along with "believing in" Jesus? Picture what it is for the little child, entering the maze of life. "Jesus Loves Me, This I Know, for the Bible Tells Me So" is a song they sing. That is childlike faith.

- What goes with maturing faith? Does it mean counting on Jesus? Does Jesus let people down? Explain.

■ Do you pray to Jesus? If so, what does that say about how you picture him? Is it a risk to believe in him?

Together

In the Gospels we hear Jesus say, "For where two or three are gathered in my name, I am there among them" (Matthew 18:20). You are likely in a group of a few more than two or three. If you are talking about growth in Christian faith, you are gathered in Jesus' name—so, if his promise is true, he must be here with you.

Some people like to "go it alone" and say that they are closest to God, to Jesus, when they are in solitude—out in the woods, looking at the ocean, at a desk in their own room.

■ What is it like when you move from "going it alone" to a group where you tell one another about some of your doubts and about your growing faith?

■ What are the circumstances that make Jesus more real to you, and when do you feel distant? Is it a risk to share this with others? How is it encouraging?

Read aloud and discuss.

Consider this

There's a familiar story of a tightrope walker who stretched his cable across the vast expanse of Niagara Falls. He walked across and back with his balancing pole as the mist of the falls sprayed all around him. Next, he walked across and back without the aid of his pole. Everyone burst into loud applause. His next trip was with a wheelbarrow. To the amazement and delight of the crowd, he went all the way across, pushing the clumsy wheelbarrow with no difficulty at all. A wide-eyed little five-year-old boy was standing near the acrobat. Suddenly, the man looked right at the boy, smiled, and said: "Son, I'm going to push this wheelbarrow back across the rope. Do you believe that I can do it?" Yes, sir, I sure do!" "You mean to tell me that you have that kind of faith in me? You really believe I can do it?" "Yeah, I really do!" said the boy. "Okay, son, get in the wheelbarrow." The boy did and the acrobat brought him safely across that tightrope and back.

■ Discuss how the actions or the boy demonstrated that he not only believed *that* the acrobat could do it but believed *in* the acrobat and his ability to carry it out right now.

- Read Matthew 11:2-6. What does it mean to take "no offense at" Jesus?

- Read Mark 2:5-10. Why were people in this story so shocked to hear that Jesus had "authority" to forgive sins?

Discovery

Acts 19:2, 6

2 [Paul] said to them, "Did you receive the Holy Spirit when you became believers?" They replied, "No, we have not even heard that there is a Holy Spirit." . . . 6 When Paul had laid his hands on them, the Holy Spirit came upon them.

Faith under construction

Paul, the great missionary who told the story of Jesus, visited Ephesus and there found some believers. He seems to have been checking up on their faith. He asked them about receiving the Holy Spirit. No, they thought, they had not, because no one had even told them about the Holy Spirit. Yet they had been baptized. As he conversed, it became clear that they were not what we would call "finished products" of faith.

Like all of us, they had to grow in faith and in experience. It helped that they were together. Would one of them, alone, have been ready to confess that something basic was missing? (Anyone who read the Scriptures would have been familiar with talk about the Holy Spirit). Would that person, alone, have done something about what was missing? It helped that Paul had spiritual discernment; he could spot what they needed to add to faith.

The Holy Spirit's reality

Whatever else we mean by the Holy Spirit, through this Spirit Jesus comes to us not as a dead figure but as a living presence. Through the Holy Spirit, the Father is with us. Through the Holy Spirit, we have gifts to use for God.

- What does it mean when you say, "I believe in the Holy Spirit?" Can the Spirit be defined, or is this a way of talking about what is real but not definable? Explain.

In John 3:8 Jesus compares the Spirit to the wind: "The wind blows where it chooses, and you hear the sound of it, but you do not know where it comes from or where it goes. So it is with everyone who is born of the Spirit."

■ Is that image helpful for your picture of the Spirit? Explain.

Consider this

The word *spirit* has come to mean something pale and shapeless, like an unmade bed. School spirit, the American spirit, the Christmas spirit, the spirit of '76, the Holy Spirit—each of these points to something you know is supposed to get you to your feet cheering but which you somehow can't rise to.

Spirit is highly contagious. When people are very excited, very happy, very sad, you can catch it from them as easily as measles or a yawn. You can catch it from what they say or from what they do or from just what happens to the air of a room when they enter it without saying or doing anything.

God also has a spirit—is Spirit, says the Apostle John (4:24). Thus God is the power of the power of life itself, has breathed and continues to breath himself into his creation. In-spires it. The spirit of God, Holy Spirit, Holy Ghost, is highly contagious (Acts 2).

From *Wishful Thinking: A Seeker's ABC*,
copyright © 1973, 1993 Frederick Buechner
(New York: HarperCollins Publishers), 110-111.

■ **Do you agree with Buechner? Explain.**

■ **For faith during seasons of risk, what do you want most from the Holy Spirit?**

A further look

■ Read 1 John 4:1-6. How do you know the spirit of truth and the spirit of error?

■ Read 1 Corinthians 6:19-20. How would you like your life to be an expression of worshiip and praise to God?

Wrap-up

See page 10 in the introduction for a description of "Wrap-up" items. See page 61 for suggested closing prayers.

Before you go, take time for the following:

- Group ministry task

- Review

- Personal concerns and prayer concerns

- Closing prayers

Daily walk

Bible readings

Day 1
Matthew 16:5-12

Day 2
Matthew 17:14-20

Day 3
Matthew 21:18-22

Day 4
Matthew 25:31-46

Day 5
Matthew 27:45-54

Day 6
Matthew 28:1-10

Day 7
Luke 18:1-8

Thought for the journey

"Faith is a living, busy, active, mighty thing, so that it is impossible for it not to be constantly doing what is good."

BC 552.11

Prayer for the journey

Help me move, O Lord, from faith that Jesus is coming to save, to faith that in his presence I am in the presence of eternal life, already begun. Amen.

Verse for the journey

"Whatever you ask for in prayer with faith, you will receive" (Matthew 21:22).

3 Faith for Seasons of Seeking

Focus

Our belief in the gospel involves the belief *that* it is true for us.

Community building

[handwritten: ask to share]

- Share a story about a person or an event that has greatly influenced what you believe.
- After the group has shared their stories, discuss what conclusions can be drawn.
- What were the stories primarily about?

    a. Dramatic experiences
    b. Respected religious leaders
    c. Personal friends and family
    d. Personal, life cycle experiences
    e. Other

[handwritten: Show goal that actually happened / listened to new testament / (during Lent last yr.) / Did it D given life]

Option

Tell about a goal in your life that was very important to you and that actually happened.

What happened and what did it mean to you?

How did it change your life in some way?

Opening prayer

O God of truth, guide our search for understanding, hope, and love, that we may grow in faith and be a blessing to those around us. Amen.

2 Timothy 1:12-13

12 I know the one in whom I have put my trust. . . .
13 Hold to the standard of sound teaching that you have heard from me, in the faith and love that are in Christ Jesus.

Ancient insights for today

When we read 2 Timothy we are, in effect, opening someone's mail and reading it. We are told that a young missionary in the early church received it from a veteran colleague. But it was clearly written so that more people than Timothy would profit from it. We do not live in the early church, but the words here are directed to us in the modern world.

Belief in / Belief that

which works best?

#1 Two kinds of faith appear in these two or three lines. The first recalls the theme that faith is "belief in . . ." It says that in Christianity, it is not *what* you know but *who* you know that matters. You can have seminary and university training, along with a Ph.D. and an encyclopedic knowledge of biblical facts, and find that it does no good in life's basic decisions. You can *#2* have childlike faith and know only the outlines of the biblical story of God's actions, and be fulfilled.

Now comes the second dimension of the faith relationship: We are to "hold to the standard of sound teaching" that was also held up for him. So we form a prayerful and personal group in order to see our faith in God reinforced, and we form a study group in order to be better informed, so that, like Timothy, we can come to some "standard of sound teaching." Christian faith is based on the gospel story, and not to know the story is to be deprived of the possibilities that faith brings.

Explore as a group.

- Suppose someone asked each of you, "What does the Christian church teach? What are the basics?" *Talk about*

- List what you think are the essentials.

Don't be embarrassed if you don't have detailed knowledge. The point is to identify things that stand out like mountains against the plains on the horizon, like skyscrapers above the city streets. As you listen to each other, see how many of the details of the essentials match. Since we are "seeking" together, building relationships along the way, see if you can be of help to each other in this task of gaining knowledge.

- How does one "gain knowledge" in the first place? If the Christian faith is based on a gospel story, where does one hear the story?

- How did you learn what you already know? Did your family, or any family, tell you the story? Did a church of your childhood, or any church? Sunday school? Vacation church school?

- Would you learn anything about the story of faith from television? Should you?

- Did you learn anything about Christian teaching from public school? Should you have?

- Was a neighbor or friend helpful in informing you?

- Timothy was a missionary and thus a "storyteller." How do we improve our ways of telling the story?

Too little knowledge of "sound teaching" can certainly be harmful to faith, since ignorance of the story of God, of Jesus, allows for no relationship to God.

- Can too much knowledge be destructive? That is, are knowledge and faith at war with each other?

- Do you know of people who are atheistic or skeptical about faith because of their reading, their study, their university education?

- Can you name learned people who are examples to the believing community for the way they express their faith? If so, talk about the value of their examples.

- Do you have models of people who combined simple "belief in" with complex "belief that". . . people who are helpful to you?

A further look

- Read Philippians 2:5-11. This reads like a hymn, a creed. What knowledge about Christ does it impart?

- Read Ephesians 6:10-17. How can knowledge become like the armor one wears?

Discovery

2 Timothy 2:1-2

1 Be strong in the grace that is in Christ Jesus; 2 and what you have heard from me through many witnesses entrust to faithful people who will be able to teach others as well.

Sharing the faith

"Pass it on." That is a key theme in Christian faith. The minute you have childlike faith, you can pass it on by telling others "what makes you tick." As you mature in faith, you can pass on more about it and more of it. Christian faith is not designed for Robinson Crusoes, alone on an island—though it sustains people who are lonely in prison or exile. Christian faith is designed for company. You get knowledge of it, and confidence for it, from others. You grow in knowledge of it, and confidence in it, when you tell others.

Faithful witnesses

Timothy was to be a "witness." He never saw Jesus with his physical eyes, nor did Paul the apostle. Yet in faith he did see, and seeing is important for anyone called to be a witness, to testify. He was a seeker who had knowledge that Jesus Christ was "raised from the dead" (2 Timothy 2:8). He trusted witnesses. We learn most from witnesses who are at risk. If someone is going to be killed for believing something, as many were in Nazi Germany or the Soviet Union, we find it important to learn what is so valuable that they will tell others, even if they will die for doing so.

Reliable witnesses

If you are a seeker, then, you know that you will be depending in part on what the gospel testifiers, the storytellers, tell about Jesus. You will gain confidence from the way Paul, who suffered hardship and was treated as a criminal, found something important to say. You will gain knowledge from what people like Timothy entrusted "to faithful people who [were] able to teach others" through the centuries. You will find yourself seeking not only to know God, but to know about the workings of God in Jesus, the Bible, the church, and the world.

Expert witnesses

Discuss as a group.

Some people in your group will probably have been on jury duty or know someone else who was. You all know stories from television dramas or books. Pool your experiences by comparing stories.

- Tell about how juries depend upon witnesses, on people who have seen something and who know something.

- How does one decide about the reliability of witnesses?

- What does an expert witness do?

■ Tell about people who know very, very much about something, who are proficient in computer games or hobbies or baseball statistics. How do they pass on their area of interest to others?

Reliable and unreliable witnesses

Think about the witnesses that brought us the story of God's actions long ago, and about those who do so now.

■ Do you know people who are "expert" at telling about what they "have heard" about the contents of the Christian faith? How do they help others?

"Avoid profane chatter" (2 Timothy 2:16) because it would lead people to impiety and bad talk. Put together a profile of the kind of person you want to be close to as you seek faith as knowledge and trust.

The other thing to talk about is what happens to our faith and knowledge of God when witnesses are not credible.

■ What do stories of clergy scandals do to the people around the offenders?

■ Can one believe the message if the messenger is an abuser? A joker? Someone who is flippant and who deals in trivia?

any one met someone that has qualities to spark your interest - church? something else?

■ What are the qualities of good Timothys in our day that lead one to be curious about the message?

In 2 Timothy 2:24, the writer of the letter wants Timothy to remind the believers who are around him "that they are to avoid wrangling over words, which . . . ruins those who are listening."

when church members argue or split

■ How does the Christian church come across to you? Do Christian teachers, leaders, and members, in your experience, "wrangle over words"?

■ If so, what do we do about this when we need to find people with whom to discuss faith?

A further look

pass on tradition

■ Read 2 Thessalonians 2:13-15. Is it a good idea to "hold fast to the traditions"? Don't traditions encrust the faith?

Read & talk about

■ Read Romans 12:3-8. By now you have discerned special gifts of the people in your study group. Identify some of the gifts of each participant.

what is your special gift?

■ Read Ephesians 1:3-10. What can be known of the mysterious will of God?" How can it be known?

2 Timothy 3:14-15

14 Continue in what you have learned and firmly believed, knowing from whom you learned it, 15 and how from childhood you have known sacred writings that are able to instruct you for salvation through faith in Christ Jesus.

A spoken faith

Christian faith, we learn from the letters to Timothy, was always in part an "oral tradition." That is, it was passed on from parent to child—Timothy's mother, Eunice, and grandmother Lois even get mentioned in this letter (2 Timothy 1:5) as people who shaped the young man. Native Americans told stories across generations and were and are an oral tradition. Jewish law is a product of oral tradition going back centuries and continuing today.

A written faith

Christian faith is also a "written tradition," which means it was and is handed down through people who read what was written. In the case of Timothy, we hear that he "learned and firmly believed" things from childhood, because from childhood he had learned "sacred writings." We call them the Hebrew Scriptures or the Old Testament, to which Christians have added the witness to Jesus in what we call the New Testament. This letter says that writings of this sort are "inspired." God breathed life into them as God did in the first human being (Genesis 2:7). They were "useful" then, and are now, "for teaching, for reproof, for correction, and for training in righteousness" (2 Timothy 3:16).

Explore and relate. *Explore* in groups of three or four; then *relate* a brief summary to the entire group.

Christian faith

Christian faith teaches what can be very practical "so that everyone who belongs to God may be proficient" (2 Timothy 3:17). It is not the case that "the more you know the better a Christian you are," but "the less you know" the less you have to draw upon as you would go about living your practical life.

- ■ What would you put into a religion that you would invent?

- ■ Would it have a God? If not, why and how would they find it attractive and "useful"? If so, what would its God be like?

- Again, if so, how would one come into relationship with God?

- How would you make a bridge from the context of God to the world of humans?

- How would you assure that the bridging would go on through the centuries?

Discuss as a group. Discuss what documents or texts do for later generations, perhaps making reference to the United States Constitution or a person's last will and testament. Now discuss what Scriptures are for in the world of seekers.

The Gideons put Bibles in hotel rooms and airplanes. Bible societies distribute Bibles free or inexpensively and leave them in all kinds of places. A nonbeliever therefore can pick one up almost anytime, anyplace. One can probably find a Bible to read in most libraries.

ask →
- Do you know of anyone who has come to faith by "stumbling upon the Bible" and reading it on her or his own?

Let's assume that most knowledge of God gained through Scriptures is passed on through the Loises and Eunices of family experience, or the Pauls of churchly experience.

- What influence does one's family or church have when determining what to believe about the Scriptures?

- Might friends, families, and acquaintances bias you against the story if they had bad experiences with it?

- Might they confuse, "snow," or delude you if others in the group had very positive experiences?

- Make a laundry list of things you'd like to "know" more about as you continue your seeking and growth in faith.

A further look

- Read 2 Peter 1:19-21. How does inspired Scripture relate to inspired holy men and women who spoke?

- Read Romans 10:14-17. Connect the act of reading Scripture to the act of preaching. Why is preaching necessary if everything is in the book?

Wrap-up

Before you go, take time for the following:

■ **Group ministry task**

■ **Review**

■ **Personal concerns and prayer concerns**

■ **Closing prayers**

Daily walk

Bible readings

Day 1
Acts 3:1-10

Day 2
Acts 6:1-6

Day 3
Acts 11:19-26

Day 4
Acts 13:4-12

Day 5
Acts 14:8-18

Day 6
Acts 15:6-21

Day 7
Acts 16:1-5

Thought for the journey

Reflect on how the role of faith works in today's church in comparison to its place in these stories, and jot down some suggestions for today's church in the light of them.

Prayer for the journey

Surround us, O God, with fellow seekers and fellow believers who can impart knowledge of faith and life, and let us become witnesses through our own growth in knowledge, grace, and courage. Amen.

Verse for the journey

"We believe that we will be saved through the grace of the Lord Jesus" (Acts 15:11).

4 Faith for Seasons of Action

Focus

God accepts you by the simple act of faith, and faith finds expression and completion in works of love.

Community building

Talk about a friendly gathering or party where you were warmly received and felt accepted by the group.

- How did it make you feel? (Good? Happy?)
- Why did you feel so accepted? (Warm handshake? Friendly smile?)
- What gifts do you have to make others feel accepted?

Option

What relational skill do you wish you were more proficient at?

Why do you value this ability?

Opening prayer

Cherishing faith, as we are coming to do, O God, help us learn that we are free to serve you and others through the acts of love. Amen.

Romans 3:28

28 We hold that a person is justified by faith apart from works prescribed by the law.

Getting right with God

Not all of us wake up in the morning ready to talk about *justification*. It is one of those words ending in "-ation" that scholars of Christianity and keepers of doctrine tend to favor, but that leave so many of us cold.

However, if we convert the question to "How do we get right with God?" the possible answers become urgent. Because if God is holy, then it is urgent to understand how we who are not naturally holy come into a right relation to God.

For understanding how we get right with God, Christians have marvelous texts in the oldest surviving Christian writings, older than the Gospels, the letters of Paul.

Paul was a great worrier; he worried lest the people he was converting or trying to convert would think that the reliable way to come into right relation with God was by doing *good works*. Who could ever be sure that the works were good enough to impress God? Would any works please God?

The importance of faith alone

Many centuries later came Protestant reformers, who were convinced that the church before their time had caused frightened, guilty people to rely on their works, which were always insufficient. So, with Paul, they proclaimed faith—*faith alone* was to be the way in which one came to be in a positive relation with God.

All people, including Christians, are tempted to justify themselves, establish their own standards for being acceptable before God, self, and others.

Explore and relate.

■ How are you tempted to feel right with God?

■ What "works" do you want to see in your life to feel justified, to feel okay and acceptable?

   a. Maintain a low-fat diet or exercise at least three times a week
   b. Prestige
   c. Power
   d. Being likeable

e. Wealth

f. Being "successful" in a particular field (work hobby, family life)

g. Other

Discuss as a group.

■ How might good deeds get in the way of faith?

■ How do you account for research that points out that even Christians tend to believe that salvation is something you deserve for living a good life and not the result of the grace of God?

Choose one of the following and explain.

    a. No one in their right mind is going to trust that something as critical as eternal salvation is out of their own control.

    b. Churches are simply responding to the public demand for motivational messages rather than the more offensive news that you cannot save yourself.

    c. The message of being justified by faith is simply too hard to grasp and accept.

    d. Paul's message of justification is not really that important to the Christian faith.

    e. It is a good example of how the self-centered nature of sin is active in us all.

    f. Other.

■ How can it be/how might it not be selfish to dwell on how each of us gets right with God?

■ All we are doing in these small group discussions is talking about faith. Is it a kind of narcissism to put so much emphasis on what faith can do for me?

Consider this

The gospel that church reformers stumbled upon in the sixteenth century is the good news that *God alone* saves people from sin, despair, and death. It is all the work of God. All we must do is believe and accept it. This simple response runs counter to our human way of doing everything. We must make some effort. We must achieve higher. We must get *ourselves* right with God. But in his writing, Luther reminds us to let "God be God." It's the special business of God to reconcile humanity. All we must do is trust God to do his saving work for us.

■ **What does the phrase "Let God be God" mean to you?**

■ **How you can let God be God in your life?**

A further look

■ Read Ephesians 2:1-10. "By grace you have been saved" (2:8). Discuss the ways in which you are tempted to be saved some other way.

■ Read Romans 4:16-25. Abraham gets credit for not mistrusting the promise. Is that a sign that he was doing good works, since he brought something to the transaction with God?

■ Read Romans 7:14-25. Do you get "wretched" from trying to please God, or is life a pretty relaxed affair?

Discovery

1 Corinthians 13:2

2 If I have all faith, so as to remove mountains, but do not have love, I am nothing.

Faith, hope, and love

We all have heard the hymn to love, 1 Corinthians 13, read at weddings. It appears on greeting cards and wall plaques. But it is not a sentimental saying. The author, the apostle Paul, had something strong and instructive in mind. He mentions at the end that, like "hope," "faith" would not always be necessary. In eternal life, in the presence of God, neither would make sense any more. But because "love" would remain, it is "the greatest" of the three (13:13).

Faith is temporary/Love will endure

What we are involved with then, in our search for faith, is a temporary quest. We might picture it as something that someday would become a souvenir, a reminiscence, an instrument of a relation to God that no longer would be necessary. But love for God and others would continue.

Faith, in other words, becomes obsolete when it turns into sight (13:12); but God is love, so love will endure. To say that, however, is not to sell faith short. Here and now we do not "see"; we walk by faith. Yet knowing that love is the greatest and most enduring expression will color our faith every day.

Discuss as a group.

What does it mean to "walk by faith, not by sight" (2 Corinthians 5:2)?

Choose one and explain.

   a. To pursue the path of love in all relationships.
   b. To stop being impressed by anyone—including ourselves—who is spiteful, selfish, or evil.
   c. To live freed to love our neighbor and love and praise God.
   d. To live as the eternal optimist.
   e. To see beyond our own needs, fears, and anger.
   f. To be open to change in one's life and environment for the sake of Jesus Christ.
   g. Other.

Faith without love (Group 1)

Divide your group into two. Have one group discuss "Faith without Love" and the other discuss "Love without Faith." Share your observations.

Describe personalities and characters who get very good at preaching and teaching the values of faith, and even get credit for it, but they lack the love that should issue from it.

Love without faith (Group 2)

Describe people who act on impulses other than the love of God in Christ, the impulses that should come with Christian faith. Should we say anything critical about the love shown by nonbelievers?

If you were hungry or unsheltered and then provided with food and shelter, would it make any difference to you whether the giver was a person of faith or not?

Tell a story of how a person's faith was made active in love. The stories can be of famous people of faith or of those you know personally. Take turns sharing stories.

What are the hazards of making too much of any one person's achievement (in a world where reputations rise and fall, as do heroines and heroes)?

Discuss as a group.

This is a good moment to connect "faith" not only with "love," but also with "hope."

Are people of hope more likely to do the works of love than those who do not have Christian hope, who do not turn to God as the power of the future? Or are they likely to be distracted by the promise of "pie in the sky by-and-by," as enemies of the Christian faith often thought that "hope of heaven" meant?

How does one who lives by faith and in hope see to it that the works of love remain high on the agenda?

A further look

- Read Hebrews 6:1-12. How can there be "perfection" in Christian life, since we remain sinners?

- Read Galatians 5:16-26. If in Christ we have crucified the flesh with its passions and desires, why is there still sin?

- Read 2 Corinthians 8:8-9. How do we become rich just because Jesus was poor?

Discovery

James 2:18

18 But someone will say, "You have faith and I have works." Show me your faith apart from your works, and I by my works will show you my faith.

Biblical check and balance

The Bible is a library and not a book. The various books in the library stress different themes, often necessarily at the expense of others. You cannot talk about everything at once. And life, including Christian life, is full of tensions, conflicting pushes and pulls, so that some of the biblical writings almost sound as balancers to others.

Faith without good actions?

So it is with the Epistle of James, written by a follower of Jesus who had enough authority to sound strong enough to balance Paul's accent on "faith without works." It is possible to stretch things so far that Paul and James seem to be in simple contradiction of each other. But it is more credible to see them accenting themes that are not easily held together. So it is with faith versus the works prescribed by the law. It is easy to take such faith and run with it.

James mentions Abraham and other spiritual ancestors, in whom "faith was active along with his works, and faith was brought to completion by the works" (James 2:22). So it is with us, though we may want to call "works" the "works of love," or just "love," as in "faith active in love."

Local needs

Explore and relate.

Use your imaginations to point to needs in your local communities, needs that can be met in part, or met better, if they are addressed by people of "faith active in love." Then have the smaller groups report to each other and find what kind of inventory has emerged.

Discuss as a group.

- How does one get started addressing the needs?

- What would you say to the kind of person James describes with obvious favor who says, "Show me your faith apart from your works"?

- Is it legitimate to do so? Is it fulfilling?

One sometimes hears people bragging about how they or their church are "better at faith" than someone else. Or you'll hear people boasting about how pure they are in their hold on and reliance upon faith. Doing so is not merely the temptation of conservative churches that stress true doctrine and pure faith. Liberal churches can do the same, when they stress that they have right ideas.

The Bible says so many good things about faith that it may seem hazardous or presumptuous to do any criticizing. But James is in the same Bible, and one can quote his writing safely and modestly.

You may want to add the issues raised to your closing prayers.

- How is his defense of good works a corrective to the person who has security in believing the right doctrines?

- What are some of your own questions or concerns regarding faith? Be willing to hear each other's issues without having to come up with answers.

Picture yourself in need

Picture yourself an exile, an innocent prisoner, someone who is hungry, someone lacking shelter, and at the same time someone who is full of doubt, despair, a sense of the lack of meaning in life, experiencing a world in which God seems silent so that you are alone. Someone comes along to hand you bread or to meet your other physical needs; someone else comes along preaching about God in Christ and the value of the gift of faith.

- Have you any idea how you would relate to each?

- How would you relate to someone who combines both of what these two "someones" claim?

Wrap-up

Before you go, take time for the following:

- **Group ministry task**

- **Review**

- **Personal concerns and prayer concerns**

- **Closing prayers**

Daily walk

Bible readings

Day 1
Hebrews 4:1-11

Day 2
Hebrews 6:1-12

Day 3
Hebrews 10:19-25

Day 4
Hebrews 11:1-16

Day 5
Hebrews 11:17-39

Day 6
Hebrews 12:1-6

Day 7
Hebrews 13:1-16.

Thought for the journey

We need the grace of God to keep together the acts of faith and the works of love, the works of love and the acts of faith.

Prayer for the journey

Let love be the priority, the first expression to issue from our faith, and help us, O Lord, to commend faith to others by showing them our love. Amen.

Verse for the journey:

"Let us hold fast to the confession of our hope without wavering, for he who has promised is faithful" (Hebrews 10:23).

5 Faith Active in Community

Focus

The faith of individuals is nurtured and challenged in the community of believers.

Community building

Describe the funniest experience you've had attending a worship service. For example, watching an active toddler wander off to another family or hearing someone snore during the pastor's sermon.

■ What does the experience teach you about the broader meaning or importance of worshiip?

Option

Share a favorite place—perhaps a secret place—where you liked to be or play alone as a child.

What did you like about your special place?

If you can't think of a childhood place, where do you like to go for solitude now?

Opening prayer

When we are alone, O God, whether by necessity or choice, instill in us an awareness of how you seek our company and would place us among companions. Help us to nurture each others' faith, O God of communion. Amen.

Matthew 18:20

20 For where two or three are gathered in my name, I am there among them.

Faith in context

We do all of our talk about faith in the context of relationships—to God, to the neighbor in need, to the unbeliever, to the fellow-believer, and, no doubt in the present case, to the fellow-seeker, who might well be represented in this group.

Christ among the faithful

It is time to lift out this "relational" aspect of faith for further examination. This text from the Gospel of Matthew gives a glimpse of life in the early church and has us overhear Jesus giving instruction to the people who were gathering in his name. Jesus does not mention faith. The verse before, however, implies it when it talks about prayer: "If two of you agree on earth on anything you ask, it will be done for you by my Father in heaven" (Matthew 18:19). Why? Because Jesus was present when people were gathered in his name. As we are.

Christ with the individual

Notice that it does not say that Jesus cannot be present to the eye and experience of faith when someone is alone. People can be shipwrecked; they can lie awake while the spouse or room-mate snores away and offers no communication; they can be in prison, or isolated in an intensive care unit, and in all cases, they can know the presence and gracious care of Jesus. God is with them.

Faith and community

Discuss as a group.

To concentrate on the aloneness of the believer, however, does not do justice at all to a consistent theme in the Bible. In one healing story, we even read that when Jesus saw "their faith," the faith of those who brought a sick person, he was impressed and he healed (Mark 2:5).

   ■ Share a time when the faith of others sustained you or someone you know.

We live in a time when many people think it best to go on their spiritual journeys alone, in solitude, away from community. They may find something, but they will have missed important elements in the fulfillment of faith—the presence of supportive companions and the vivid experience of Christ.

- How has the support of others been a valuable part of your faith group?

- How has time alone been a valuable part of your faith life?

These days people talk more about wanting to be "spiritual" or to have "spirituality" than to be "faithful" or to have "faith." One of the reasons seems to be that spirituality is marketable as a goal one can acquire alone—just as one can do weight lifting or body-building alone—whereas faith belongs to community, and many reject community. Many people will say something like, "I am very spiritual, but I don't have faith in a Christian God, and I don't like organized religion, and I certainly have no use for the church."

- Why do so many speak that way today?

- Is there something about the culture around the church that promotes it?

- What is it about the church and about "organized religion" that helps criticism of them make sense?

- What is it about the Christian faith that makes it tempting to avoid being with the Christian community?

Choose one and explain.

    a. God's will is more important than my will.

    b. The call to be a servant of others, including those I may not want to serve.

    c. Christian growth includes daily repentance.

    d. A call to financial stewardshiip.

    e. The Christian faith accepts suffering as part of the path of love and faithfulness.

    f. Worship traditions that are hard to follow or simply difference from the tradition I grew up with.

    g. There are so many different expressions of the Christian faith.

    h. Other.

- What do your answers to that question tell you about your own search for faith, or for deeper faith?

Picture a setting where your search for faith might be deepened—an empty cathedral, a mountain, a lake. Picture a setting that suggests your faith might be strengthened in company—the face of people in need, saints, a great revival.

■ Do people of different personalities find different ways and places?

A further look

■ Read Hebrews 12:1-2. How do we experience a "cloud of witness" to keep us in faith?

■ Read 1 Corinthians 12:12-26. How do those of us who make up this group begin to reveal ourselves as having different gifts in the body of Christ?

■ Read 1 John 1:5-10. Discuss how the fellowship we have with God in Christ is connected to the fellowship we have with each other.

Discovery

Psalm 111:1

1 **Praise the LORD!**
I will give thanks to the LORD
with my whole heart,
in the company of the upright,
in the congregation.

Reading the Psalms

The Christian faith takes root on the soil of the stories and pictures of God in the Hebrew Scriptures that Christians call the Old Testament. One of the great experiences of people who read that book is an encounter with the book of praise called the Psalms.

A book of praise

Again and again the Psalms picture people of faith engaging in an act called "praise." In fact, Psalm 111 begins with a short line that one hears, sometimes too often these days by people who are casual about it (and even answer the phone with it as a routine greeting): "Praise the Lord!" Yet the impulse behind saying "Praise the Lord!" is a proper one, and one does well to think about what praise does for faith—just as what praying does (as we saw in Matthew 18:19-20). In other words, people do not grow in faith just by talking about it. They grow by doing things together that both demand faith and contribute to its growth. Like praying, in Matthew; like praising, as in the Psalms.

Praising God together

The psalmist calls the congregation that praises together "the company of the upright." He had in mind the Old Testament picture of how one became upright: You became part of a people created by the promises and work of God; you became part of a covenant. God acted with gracious care and steadfast love to create and keep gathering and healing this people. You were saved "as a people" and not as a lonely seeker. God acted favorably toward Israel as God acts favorably toward the church, the gathering, the congregation who in faith becomes the new "company of the upright."

Discuss as a group.

■ What does praising God in the company of the upright do for the growth of faith?

It has been pointed out that almost everything "the congregation" does, someone or something else can do: They can have committees, print a newsletter, have programs for the homeless, meet in conventions. What is unique with the believing community is that it praises God.

■ What can be done to assure that worship, the praise of God, the action of a congregation, contributes to faith?

■ Share with each other descriptions of places and experiences of worship that "turned you off" or "turned you on."

   a. What went on in one setting that made everything look routine and maybe even hypocritical?

   b. What went on in another setting that led to an experience of the presence of God, a desire to return?

Together, come up with some ideas.

■ What would you tell a worship committee it should do to help make possible a richer setting in which God can choose to make the presence felt?

Some may want to talk about the psychology of praise-in-the-congregation and the growth of faith. One modern Christian said, "I kiss my child because I love her and I kiss my child in order to love her." That is, even when the parent did not feel like reaching out with a gesture of love, doing so helped one "feel more like it." The same may be true between marital partners.

■ Is it a bit showy and hypocritical to make the gesture—or do the ritual—in order to "feel more like it"? Explain.

We also know something about mob psychology: You can be part of a crowd scene and get carried away and start believing things you did not believe before. You might sing the praises of "good old alma mater" even if you did not go there, just because those around you are doing so. So it may be that the company of those around you praising God might contribute to the psychology of group membership and the illusion of a growth in faith. Or it can be a legitimate aid to the seeker?

- What are the dangers as well as benefits of public worship with others?

A further look

- Read Exodus 4:27-31. How does the faith of "the elders" connect with "the people" who believed?

- Read Hebrews 11:8-12. How does the faith of Abraham relate to the experience and faith of many descendants?

- Read Ephesians 1:15-22. How is growth in faith dependent upon the existence of the church?

Discovery

Acts 11:23-24

23 When [Barnabas] came and saw the grace of God, he rejoiced, and he exhorted them all to remain faithful to the Lord with steadfast devotion; 24for he was a good man, full of the Holy Spirit and of faith. And a great many people were brought to the Lord.

Building up faith

Talk as much as we might about how faith is experienced and developed in community, we have to remember that communities and congregations are made up of individuals, each of them different, all of them capable of building up faith or letting it wear down. An individual can have great impact on the growth of community and the deepening of congregational life.

The roots of faith building

In the book of Acts, our best picture of early Christian congregational life, we hear of the church at Antioch, the third biggest metropolis in the Roman Empire, and the place where believers were first called Christians. Believers fled there when the church at Jerusalem began to be persecuted. Some of the people there were from Cyprus, so a disciple named Barnabus, also a Cypriot, was sent there to preach.

Barnabus had an immediate impact on the community. He did not come with proofs for the existence of God or 23 historians' arguments to certify that Jesus' tomb was empty on Easter morning. No, he told what God had done for him in the community of believers; he told the story personally. And since they were attracted to him because he was good, and full of faith, and moved by the Spirit, he both helped those already in faith grow more faithful and he helped the circle of believers grow.

Discuss as a group.

Consider this

Some people think that faith connects with scientific certitude. Thus, in the case of the Shroud of Turin, an old linen that has a mysterious image on it, one that some think bears the marks of Christ's body and thus might have been his grave cloth, some say: If science can prove that it comes from the time of Christ and the place of the crucifixion and resurrection, many will believe.

But one must ask: If that is the case, why would not the disciples, who would have had it, not run around the various lands saying, "He is risen, and this cloth proves it"? No, they sent Barnabas, and many believed.

■ What is the difference between "scientific proof" and the message Barnabas brought?

■ What are some of the things that you think might help other people come to faith or that might increase yours? Philosophical proofs for the existence of God? Archaeological evidence that helps certify the accuracy of historical scenes in the Bible? Or people?

■ What examples can be given of something said or done in this group that contributed to faith?

■ Now give an example of a person who helped. (Don't worry about flattering someone; we are all struggling here together, and whoever gets referred to will quickly shrug off the word and not order a Certificate of Faith-building Influence.)

■ Paint a verbal portrait of "the good person," "the person full of the Holy Spirit and of faith," in order to isolate features that tell us how we might be and act in faith.

A further look

■ Read Thessalonians 1:2-10. What examples of community do you see in churches today?

■ Read Acts 2:37-47. What is there about this account of the life of the early church that you would like to see emphasized in the church today?

Wrap-up

Before you go, take time for the following:

- Group ministry task

- Review

- Personal concerns and prayer concerns

- Closing prayers

Daily walk

Bible readings

Day 1
Psalm 1:1-6

Day 2
Psalm 8:1-9

Day 3
Psalm 27:1-14

Day 4
Psalm 130:1-8

Day 5
Psalm 131:1-3

Day 6
Psalm 139:1-18

Day 7
Psalm 141:1-10

Thought for the journey

Words like *believe* and *belief* and *faith* do not appear in a book like the Psalms, but the concept of faithful reliance on God through thick and thin runs through it.

Prayer for the journey

Help us each experience a growth in character, O Lord, so that we can credibly commend the faith to those who come into contact with us.

Verse for the journey

"I praise you, for I am fearfully and wonderfully made" (Psalm 139:14).

6 Faith for the Season of Victory

Faith has limits, and yet faith offers us limitless possibilities.

Community building

Have each member share examples of outstanding individuals who beat the odds or overcame great obstacles to succeed in life. For example: Helen Keller, Jesse Owens, Martin Luther King, Jr.

- What do these examples tell us about the limitless possibilities of faith?

- Tell about one area of your life where the inspiration of such people can be a positive influence.

Option

Share a valued understanding of Christian faith that has emerged from your exploration of faith with this small group.

How can this understanding influence your individual life/your life with others?

Opening prayer

In our times of discouragement and disappointment, if not doubt and despair, visit us with your Spirit, O Lord, and strengthen our faith, for you have already given us the victory. Amen.

1 John 5:4-5

[4] Whatever is born of God conquers the world. And this is the victory that conquers the world, our faith. [5] Who is it that conquers the world but the one who believes that Jesus is the Son of God?

The relevance of faith

Faith is for many different kinds of seasons: For times of struggle when one wrestles with doubt or suffering. For seasons of joy, as when a child is born, when everything seems to work, when one experiences love—and yet is haunted by the awareness that all these have limits and will not satisfy all the desires and needs of the heart. For seasons in which one experiences contradictions—highs and lows, doubts mixed with faith, bitter sweetness and sweet bitterness. It begins with childlikeness, and moves one, through growth in grace, to maturity, and ends—with death.

The limits of faith

"It ends." That is the hard word to write and to read, the difficult reality about which to think. When we are serious, we do not welcome the prospect of endings. We may be bored by slow-paced developments, by scenes in which nothing happens. But we fear closures, slammings of doors, turnings of last pages, and the prospect of the spade of earth on the grave. "It ends—with death." One asks: what good is faith if it follows the same sequence of a human life and ends with death?

The triumph of faith

The New Testament writings are unanimous: Faith ends with death because it is no longer needed. Only love endures into eternity. But the writer of one of the books near the end of the New Testament, the author of 1 John, shares the other unanimous proclamation of the New Testament writings: Death itself is not the end. Faith is "born of God," and "whatever is born of God conquers the world." That means a world in which endings and death have their place. Faith "conquers" these; faith "conquers the world." Being God's gift, it lives as long as God does, wherever God does. Eternally.

Three features

Divide into three groups; each take one of the three terms and create a list of examples.

■ It is said that we live our lives marked by three features. Divide into three groups and each group take one of these three terms and create a list of examples.

    a *Finitude*—everything has limits and dies
    b. *Contingency*—accidents happen
    c. *Transience*—things pass away through time

The act of identifying what it is that is finite, what is contingent, what is transient—shown from examples of our life—is itself an affirmative step. Someone in the first group may speak of the death of a child; in the second, of an auto accident or a disease that came without our having done wrong to our body; in the third, of a house fire that consumed the children's baby pictures. Let there be narratives to go with these.

Come together and share summaries from the three groups.

■ Where does faith come in?

■ As a whole group, select some of these and illustrate what faith might look like in the context of each case. Discuss whether it produces illusions and evasions and escapes—or is there something realistic about faith, when someone introduces it as the element that conquers the world, including finitude, contingency, and transience.

Practice giving advice to each other.

■ Take one or another of the situations and share advice that would *not* help. Your list will grow long.

    a. The loss of the child is not too bad.

    b. Just have faith, knowing that she is with Jesus.

    c. Evidently the Lord saw reason not to protect your friend and let the train hit her.

    d. Faith will take care of everything, and time heals, so you will eventually see God's purpose.

Respond to the lists created by the three groups.

    e. Other.

■ Practice saying *appropriate* things about faith in the face of life's tougher circumstances, or have some participants tell what helped them when they heard of a faith that conquers the world.

A further look

■ Read John 5:24. Why does Jesus say the believer *has* eternal life, not *will have* eternal life?

■ Read 2 Corinthians 5:1-7. "We walk by faith, not by sight." Is there no sight on this side of eternity? Do we get glimpses? Explain.

Romans 8:38-39

[38] For I am convinced that neither death, nor life, nor angels, nor rulers, nor things present, nor things to come, nor powers, [39]nor height, nor depth, nor anything else in all creation, will be able to separate us from the love of God in Christ Jesus our Lord.

The promise of eternal fellowship

We connect with "the love of God in Christ Jesus our Lord" through faith, and faith connects God with us, since faith is God's gift. So these words that do not mention belief or faith point directly to it.

The promise in its original context

The author, Paul, was someone who had already experienced many of the events and items mentioned in those few lines. He lived in a world in which Christians were highly aware of hostile "powers" that engaged in battle against them from unseen worlds. But he also lived in a world in which these forces were embodied in kings and emperors, destroyers of faith, and tempters.

What can separate us from God's love?

Some commentators have noticed that although Paul said that "things present" and "things to come" would not separate us from the love of God in Christ, he did not say "things past." That is significant, because from the past comes guilt, our sense of failing, the cause of despair, the record of broken relationships and unkept promises, and these can be so haunting that they might separate us from the love of God in Christ. No, Paul implies and often says elsewhere: God took care of the past, too, in sending Christ. Those who in faith and repentance accept what God gives in Christ have no reason to be separated from God's love—in the past, present, or future.

Explore and relate.

We do worry, however, about today and tomorrow—how do we know that a bigger test is not ahead?

■ What could happen in the future that would tempt us to forget the gifts from seasons of joy?

In Paul's experience, certified by millions after him, however, it is precisely in such times of testing that we can see that the love of God will not be denied, and that faith can grasp the promises and experiences that come along with it.

The unseen world

We have been so eager thus far to talk about the place of faith in our day-to-day ordinary relationships, that we may have flattened out and reduced the biblical picture. We tend to deal with the seen world. What about the unseen?

Discuss as a group.

Consider this

Angels are "big" these years, and more people believe in the existence of evil angels, devils, than did some years ago (whether or not more believe in God!). There are people who say we will never understand the evils of Hitlerism or Stalinism or Maoism or the mafia down the block unless we see them representing the "personalities and powers" that oppose the will of God. Still others say that national or military or corporate life, or the worlds of entertainment and media are superhumanly powerful and that they may lead us from the weak and childlike things about which faith speaks.

■ Which approach strengthens your faith the most?

   a. Attention to the unseen world.
   b. A focus on issues that are practical and earthbound.

Tell short stories about relatives or friends who evidenced deeper faith through crisis, when there would have been good reason to deny faith—thus cutting a person off from the love of God in Christ. Engage in cautious critique or open support of these stories, taking care not to violate someone else's interpretation of what went on in his or her life.

■ Have you seen someone lose faith because she or he was not attending to it? That means *not* listening to the Word, reading the Bible, praying, attending worship.

■ Have you seen someone lose faith because the burdens of life that test faith were too strong?

■ Both can happen, but which form of loss of faith do you think is more prevalent, and why?

■ What can you learn about your faith from the answers you and this group give to such a question?

A further look

- Read Hebrews 11:13-16. How do you picture "the city" that God has prepared for us?

- Read Isaiah 25:6-10. Does the fact that God will wipe away all tears have anything to do with our tears, here and now?

- Read 1 Corinthians 12:20-26. How does the suffering of one of us lead to suffering of others? How can the honoring of one of us lead to rejoicing of all of us?

Discovery

Philippians 3:10-11

10 I want to know Christ and the power of his resurrection and the sharing of his sufferings by becoming like him in his death, 11 if somehow I may attain the resurrection from the dead.

A complete understanding

Several chapters ago we talked about the difference between "belief in" and "belief that" and no doubt drew some conclusions that faith has a dimension of knowledge—it is not all experience—and knowledge has a dimension of faith—it is not all pure reason. But this text and this final theme push the limits further.

In this letter to Philippians, Paul speaks of knowledge as a final fulfillment of faith. Here is a language for the seasons of completion, of fulfillment.

An eternal knowledge

The Apostles' Creed ends with words that say "I believe in . . . the resurrection of the body, and the life everlasting." Someone has said that if you start with the words "I believe in God," you have to end with "the life everlasting." Otherwise you are not talking about the God of Christian faith, a God of love who would never break off relations, would never let the divine love end just because of the physical death of the beloved on earth.

Knowledge of divine fellowship

Paul does not paint this picture of faith-as-knowledge in rose, pastel, and evasive terms. One shares "the power of [Christ's] resurrection and the sharing of his sufferings." Our faith lets us share, already now, in something of the power of the resurrection, even as it calls us to reenter the world in which one suffers with and for Christ and the people for whom Christ died.

■ Why do you think Paul has the sequence (a)"I want to know the power of his resurrection" and then (b) "and the sharing of his sufferings"? Didn't his sufferings come first, and then his resurrection? Don't ours?

People talk about eternal life with God in many different terms. At a funeral or memorial service one might hear words of comfort that point to any number of these.

a. Resurrection of the body
b. Immortality of the soul
c. Mansions above
d Heaven
e. The New Jerusalem
f. Omega (the last word in the Greek alphabet)
g. Christ, the consummation
g. Other

There is no need to limit imagination, since we lack the mind of God or direct knowledge of what eternal life as a completion, a consummation of faith might mean. Putting premature limits on the imaginings or making fun of what someone else pictures may well do an injustice.

Describe an image of eternal life that is most helpful to you.

■ What it is about any or all of these images that fits with the pictures of faith that we have developed?

■ Should we replace some long-imagined pictures with some we acquire later? Do you? Explain.

A further look

■ Read Romans 10:9-17. Why is it so important to believe not only in God, in Jesus, but in the reality that God raised Jesus from the dead?

■ Read Philippians 1:19-26. Picture ways in which Christ is exalted in our bodies.

■ Read 1 Corinthians 15:12-19. How is life different when we keep the resurrection of Christ in view?

Wrap-up

Before you go, take time for the following:

■ Group ministry task

■ Review

■ Personal concerns and prayer concerns

■ Closing prayers

Daily walk

Bible readings

Day 1
Isaiah 2:2-4

Day 2
Isaiah 9:1-7

Day 3
Isaiah 10:20-27

Day 4
Isaiah 11:1-10

Day 5
Isaiah 26:1-15

Day 6
Isaiah 32:1-8

Day 7
Isaiah 35:1-10

Thought for the journey

Despite the many challenges of life, nothing can separate us from God's love in Christ Jesus. This promise is for our past, our present, and our future.

Prayer for the journey

O Lord, let the power of the resurrected life show through the doings of our ordinary life in the here and now. We pray in the name of the risen Christ. Amen.

A verse for the journey

"They shall beat their swords into plowshares, and their spears into pruning hooks; nation shall not lift up sword against nation, neither shall they learn war any more" (Isaiah 2:4b).

Appendix

Record information about group members here.

Names	Addresses	Phone Numbers

Group commitments

"Do not be conformed to this world, but be transformed by the renewing of your minds, so that you may discern what is the will of God—what is good and acceptable and perfect" (Romans 12:2).

■ For our time together, we have made the following commitments to each other

■ Goals for our study of this topic are

■ Our group ministry task is

■ My personal action plan is

Prayer requests

Prayers

■ Closing Prayer

Lord God, you have called your servants
to ventures of which we cannot see the
ending, by paths as yet untrodden,
through perils unknown. Give us faith to
go out with good courage, not knowing
where we go, but only that your hand is
leading us and your love supporting us;
through Jesus Christ our Lord. Amen.

From *Lutheran Book of Worship* (page 153) copyright © 1978.

■ The Lord's Prayer

(If you plan to use the Lord's Prayer, record the version your group uses in the next column.)

Resources

■ Books

Bonhoeffer, Dietrich. *The Cost of Discipleship.* New York: Macmillan, 1983.

This book is based on the Sermon on the Mount; it includes many reflections on the nature of faith.

King, Martin Luther Jr. *A Testament of Hope.* New York: HarperCollins, 1986.

This book talks as much about faith as about hope in this collection of the civil rights leader's writings through the years.

Lewis, C. S. *Mere Christianity.* New York: Macmillan, 1986.

Here is a work that has patently led many to faith in recent decades.

Lull, Timothy, ed. *Martin Luther's Basic Theological Writings.* Philadelphia: Fortress Press, 1989.

There are few pages that do not deal directly with themes bearing on the subject of faith.

Brown, Charles C., compiler, *Reinhold Niebuhr Reader: Selected Essays, Articles, and Book Reviews.* Philadelphia: Trinity Pr. International, 1992.

Here is a collectopm of writings of a notable American theologian who was mainly interested in applying faith to the world of power and daily life.

Tillich, Paul. *The Courage to Be.* New Haven: Yale Univ. Press, 1952.

This is difficult to read but is one of the more profound essays connecting theology and psychology in our time.

Please tell us about your experience with INTERSECTIONS.

4. What I like best about my INTERSECTIONS experience is

5. Three things I want to see the same in future INTERSECTIONS books are

6. Three things I might change in future INTERSECTIONS books are

7. Topics I would like developed for new INTERSECTIONS books are

8. Our group had _____ sessions for the six chapters of this book

9. Other comments I have about INTERSECTIONS are

Thank you for taking the time to fill out and return this questionnaire.

---------------------FOLD CARD IN HERE, SEAL WITH TAPE, AND MAIL TODAY!----------------------

Please check the INTERSECTIONS book you are evaluating.

☐ Following Jesus   ☐ Death and Grief   ☐ Men and Women
☐ The Bible and Life   ☐ Divorce   ☐ Peace
☐ Captive and Free   ☐ Faith   ☐ Praying
☐ Caring and Community   ☐ Jesus: Divine and Human   ☐ Self-Esteem

Please tell us about your small group.

1. Our group had an average attendance of _____ .

2. Our group was made up of
_____ Young adults (19-25 years)
_____ Adults (most between 25-45 years)
_____ Adults (most between 45-60 years)
_____ Adults (most between 60-75 years)
_____ Adults (most 75 and over)
_____ Adults (wide mix of ages)
_____ Men (number) and _____ women (number)

3. Our group (answer as many as apply)
_____ came together for the sole purpose of studying this INTERSECTIONS book.
_____ has decided to study another INTERSECTIONS book.
_____ is an ongoing Sunday school group.
_____ met at a time other than Sunday morning.
_____ had only one facilitator for this study.

BUSINESS REPLY MAIL

FIRST-CLASS MAIL   PERMIT NO. 22120   MINNEAPOLIS, MN

POSTAGE WILL BE PAID BY ADDRESSEE

Augsburg Fortress
ATTN INTERSECTIONS TEAM
PO BOX 1209
MINNEAPOLIS MN 55440-8807